Ten Things New Teachers Need To Succeed

Robin Fogarty

PEARSON
SkyLight
Glenview, Illinois

Ten Things New Teachers Need to Succeed

Published by Pearson Professional Development
1900 E. Lake Ave., Glenview, IL 60025
800-348-4474 or 847-657-7450
Fax 847-486-3183
info@skylightedu.com
http://www.skylightedu.com

ISBN 1-57517-379-4

2828D-McN

Z Y X W V U T S R Q P O N M L K J I H G F E D
08 07 06 05 04 15 14 13 12 11 10 9 8 7 6 5

SkyLight Professional Development

Dedication

I dedicate this book,
with love,
to my only son,
Timothy,
who became
my teacher
this past year,
teaching me more
about who I am
than I could ever
have imagined.

Acknowledgments

I want to acknowledge the "newest" teachers I have had the privilege to know for their honest conversations, genuine frustrations and willingness to grow:

Tiffany Fegley Krubert, formerly of Pritzker School, Chicago Public Schools; currently at home with "Baby Jack."

Kathy Dopp, fifth grade teacher and mentor and coach for the "Olympics of the Mind" championship team; Canajoharie School District, Canajoharie, New York.

Molly Moynihan, formerly of Senn High School, Chicago Public Schools; currently teaching journalism at Evanston Township High School, Evanston, Illinois.

Esme Raji Codell, formerly of the Chicago Public Schools; currently author, activist, and advocate for the teacher's voice.

Preface

Having agreed to "write a little book for new teachers" for SkyLight, my publisher of many years, I tried to recall the things new teachers had said to me over the years. I sat down to list my ideas for the ten things I thought teachers needed, both to succeed and to stay in the profession. I wanted to see if I could actually list *just* ten things.

I was joyful in the task and rendered my thoughts on paper as fast as I could type them. I knew I had hit the mother lode. I had discovered a way to expose the heart and soul of this time-honored gift called teaching. I had said these things many times before as I talked with teachers around the world, about the art and science of the act of teaching.

My wish for you—the reader, the new teacher, the old teacher, the math teacher, the music teacher, the favorite teacher, the remembered teacher, the substitute teacher or the "second career" teacher—is that my words speak to you and your teaching; that they guide you and inspire you to continue with this very important work called *teaching.*

A challenge from my constructivist grounding that I just cannot resist, is to invite you, the reader, to note the ten things you would put on the list. Then, as you read, you'll have the fun of seeing how well your thinking meshed or matched with mine.

1.

2.

3.

4.

5.

6.

7.

8.

9.

10.

Enjoy!

—Robin Fogarty

Contents

Introduction

I am a teacher. I've been a teacher for over thirty years, knowing from the time I was ten that teaching was what I was going to do. Like many new teachers who are reading this book, I love children and gravitate to them and them to me. I love the act of creating, of inventing, of writing. Like so many teachers, I am a people person who likes to be in the midst of the action (an appropriate gift for the those who choose to be in a room with thirty busy ones) and I am well-schooled in the art and science of teaching.

My Bachelor of Arts in Early Childhood/Elementary Education is from State University of New York at Potsdam (S.U.N.Y.), my Masters of Arts in Instructional Strategies is from National-Louis University in Evanston, Illinois, and my Doctorate of Philosophy in Curriculum and Instruction and Human Resource Development is from Loyola University at Chicago.

My vision of this little book is one of high aspirations. I see it sitting beside the great "little books" of my lifetime, such as Strunk and White's *Elements of Style,* Robert Pirsig's *Zen and the Art of Motorcycle Maintenance,* and Laurence Peter's *Peter's Quotations: Ideas for Our Time.* These are the texts that fit the spirit of my vision.

I see my book becoming the well-worn desk copy, the quick reference, the on-hand authority for new and renewing teachers. I see tattered pages of yellowed paper, crimped corners and underlinings of favorite passages revisited again and again. I see teachers sharing and comparing their originals with the new editions to check for any discrete changes or to see if the new copy is really any different than that familiar old version treasured for so many years.

I hope this little book will become a cherished companion that is savored by seasoned staff and bestowed upon new graduates as the quintessential "gift to give." I see this little book as my gift to the profession . . . a giving back, if you will, to the courageous ones who strive to teach. It is, in my eyes, both a way of previewing the skills of teaching, and perhaps more importantly, a way of renewing the spirit of those who teach.

While not written as a detailed "how-to," *Ten Things A New Teacher Needs* serves to open the conversation among educators ripe for dialogue about the intricacies of a complex profession. Some might see this book as a checklist of sorts that profiles the critical areas of teaching expertise.

The book's intended audience is preservice teachers who are just learning about teaching methodology, new teachers preparing for their first teaching position, substitute teachers working their way into a first full-time position, or experts entering the profession as second career teachers. *Ten Things A New Teacher Needs* is a "slice of life" in the world of the teacher.

A Knowing Colleague as Counsel . . . About the Policies, Practices, and the Politics!

Without a doubt, a number one priority for the new teacher is to have a friend in the school, a knowing colleague on staff who is there for the "new kid on the block." After many conversations with first and second year teachers (some who made it and others who chose to leave teaching within their first few years), I've noticed teachers invariably talk about the need for someone they can count on, someone they can go to when they have questions and when they need help.

While many districts have established formal "new teacher induction programs" that include an assigned mentor for each new teacher, the reality is that not all schools have the resources to do this. Therefore, with the prediction of two and a half million new teachers entering the field over the next ten years and the growing exodus of "seasoned staff" into the world of retirement, it seems wise advice for new teachers to assume responsibility for finding that someone they need: that friend, that coach, that mentor.

PROACTIVELY SEEK A MENTOR

In other words, new teachers can't wait for someone to be assigned as mentor or for a friend to emerge from the ranks. They must proactively seek out a caring colleague. They must find someone who exhibits qualities they admire—a solid knowledge base, a sense of humor, or a manner of working with the students. It must be someone who resonates with them and their core values. They must find someone who is right for them as well as someone who is available and accessible when they need help.

They must find someone familiar with district policies, who understands how the district runs the testing program and knows what to do with the mountain of memos that come from central office. They need to find someone who knows how to work within the current and accepted practices regarding required textbooks and the accepted role of academic freedom in the district.

New teachers must find someone familiar with building practices who knows how to get around the school and the grounds. New teachers must find someone who understands the rules and "regs" of accepted practices regarding lunchtime, recess, study hall, absences, discipline, report cards, parent calls, internet use, and other things that occur regularly in the day of the classroom teacher.

The novice needs to find someone who knows the politics of the school faculty. Who knows what and whom? Who gets things done and who blocks things from getting done? Who are the informal leaders and how much power do they really have? Who is most likely to welcome the role of coach or mentor? Whom do they want as their friend and knowing colleague?

A Place Called "My Room" for Students to Grow, to Groom, and to Zoom!

In a place called school is the place called "my room." This room, the classroom, is considered sacred territory to teachers. It is their proclaimed domain and the room projects the beliefs, values, and the personality of the teacher residing within. Teachers know this to be true: "The classroom is that teacher's room!" It is an extension of who that teacher is. It speaks of the teacher's education and training, philosophies, priorities, and passions. It speaks to the students teachers teach and the parents they meet.

CREATE A CLIMATE THAT FOSTERS GROWTH AND PRIDE

If the room presents a rich environment, genuine student involvement results. It should demonstrate that richness in black and white—and greens and reds and yellows—in maps and charts and potted plants, in bulletin boards, student supplies, science equipment, computer gear, and student desks and chairs. If the room speaks of student papers, works of art, time for thinking deeply, pondering and puzzling, then this room speaks of the teacher's expectations for the students who call this place "my room."

If the room evokes a rigorous learning climate where effort is applauded, a challenging culture where risk is expected, and a protected zone of emotional safety where every student feels respected and honored and included, then surely it is a room that invites learners to grow emotionally as well as intellectually.

If the room inspires peak performances for every learner to become all he or she is capable of becoming, if it inspires habits of mind for precision in work, persistence in effort, and perfection in performance, then surely this is the place for students to excel, each in his or her own way.

The classroom is the place where students can grow and groom and zoom. The words "my room" evoke a feeling of pride in the teacher and the students who know it well from the inside out. Remember, it is in this room that students develop intellectually. It is the place where they "prune and groom" physically, and it is the place where they "zoom" as individuals in peak performance for every encounter. Teachers understand that the term "my room" doesn't really mean their room but, rather, the students' room. It is the place where it all happens that year and it is up to the teacher to design with forethought and care for the eventful occasions that are sure to occur.

A Method for Managing 1,500 Decisions: On Your Seat/On Your Feet!

It has been said that a classroom teacher makes 1,500 decisions in a day. Some of those decisions are "on your seat" decisions that occur in the quiet moments of planning and plotting the course of action—or the reaction. Other decisions are "on your feet" decisions that occur in the heat of the action, when the dust has not yet settled and a teacher's mind is on any number of things all at once. A method for managing this multitude of decisions is the only way for sanity to prevail. It is not a method, but many methods for doing things that mix and match with myriad things that need doing.

Included in the category of "on your seat" decisions are schedules, charts, and calendars, units of study, lesson plans, and weekly quizzes. Teachers need a one-page schedule that depicts their responsibilities for day-to-day occurrences. They need a calendar of events that plots the weekly and monthly happenings. Teachers need posters and bulletin boards that bring the notes and the news into their rooms. They need a seating chart—in pencil, as it may change frequently. Teachers need a planning book to document in writing the upcoming curriculum units and their detailed daily lesson plans. They need a grade book to record the grades needed to give the final grade and they need a notebook to note last-minute changes that make each day a different day than originally planned.

LET COMMON SENSE RULE THE MOMENT OF DECISION

In the category of "on your feet" decisions are any number of things that erupt and disrupt the day. Throughout the day, a teacher's radar is up for the waves of data they must detect. Teachers must decide who is bored or challenged or frustrated and what plans of action to employ to "move" each student forward. Teachers must decide how much or how little to review or reboot from the previous day's lesson, or how hard or how easy to make Friday's pop quiz. Teachers must decide, in the midst of the front line action, who to move for more challenge in reading or math and who to move for in-depth review. Teachers must decide, on the spot, whose story is reliable and who is liable. They must intervene and convene on a moment's notice. Teachers must decide any number of things in the course of a day, and to do this with wisdom and wit is no easy task. The best bet is to observe and assess situations as best one can and let common sense rule the moment of decision. Later reflection can usually rectify a regrettable decision.

A Discipline Plan That Works on Paper and on Students!

An often troublesome factor for the new teacher involves student discipline. From the moment they leave for school until long after the final bell sounds, students are interacting passively, assertively, or aggressively. Dealing with discipline decisions can be the most time-consuming part of the job in those early years of teaching.

Discipline problems range from the daily squabbles of younger students (fighting on the playground over who owns the ball and who goes first) to the bothersome pranks of rambunctious teens (creating graffiti on the building or mercilessly teasing the girls) to chronic tardiness, absenteeism, and to escalating violence.

There is no way to bypass this part of the teaching scene but there are ways to lighten the load of disciplinary concerns for the new teacher. The first line of defense is to establish a written discipline plan that is clearly posted for all to see and to heed. The written plan delineates the rules of the classroom and, ideally, the consequences for breaking the rules. As the teacher orchestrating the development of the discipline plan, keep in mind that "Less is more!" Keep the number of rules manageable by limiting the rules to priority concerns: safety of the students, fairness for all, and work ethics that spell success. This classroom discipline plan may be created with or without student input. Some feel it is better for students to have a say so they feel ownership of the plan and are therefore more likely to respect and adhere to the agreements made. Whatever the method of development, the plan needs to align with the district and school policies, and it must be shared explicitly with the students and the parents.

BE CONSISTENT! BE FLEXIBLE!

The second line of defense in handling student discipline is not as neat and tidy as the first. This second concern is the reaction of the teacher when the infraction is actually occurring, or the response of the teacher immediately after a problem surfaces. The advice often given by the discipline gurus is to *be consistent* and, at the same time, to *be flexible.* At first glance, this message seems contradictory. How can a teacher be consistent and flexible at the same time? Upon further examination this message does contain some seeds of wisdom in dealing with the "human factor." The teacher must be consistent in terms of interpreting the rules and consequences and the teacher needs to know when to ask for help: a *social worker* for a constantly tired, hungry student; the *principal* for the student who will not obey posted rules or whose parents won't respond to requests or inquiries; *security* if a student has a weapon. At the same time, the teacher also needs to be flexible in understanding and allowing for extenuating circumstances and individual factors. In other words, always factor in the human factor! Use your best judgment and manage the incident with the least amount of distraction from the lesson and the least amount of focus on the violator. Don't feed into his or her conscious or subconscious need for attention. Use common sense and trust your plan. Students inherently want to know what the parameters are, and they respect the rules of the classroom if they are consistently enforced.

A Standard Understanding of the Almighty Standards!

A standard understanding of the standards is definitely "the standard" for teachers in contemporary schools. Standards delineate the student achievement goals of the curriculum. Now, hear this: Standards are not the curriculum. They are the goals of the curriculum. Teachers don't teach the standards, they teach the curriculum and, in the process, they help students achieve the standards. For example, if the standard states that "All students are able to communicate effectively in written and oral communication," the teaching of the communication skills may be accomplished through work with their interpretation of *The Red Badge of Courage.* Or the skills may be addressed through a science curriculum in which students prepare a written and oral presentation of a genetic disease. In both scenarios, the standard of effective communication is clustered with standards in other areas. It can be one of the overriding goals, but in one case the curriculum centers around the study of a novel, and in the other situation the curriculum focuses on the study of a biology unit.

"CLUSTER" STANDARDS INTO CURRICULUM CONTENT

The real concern for teachers is in the knowledge and understanding of the standards—knowing the accepted and established content priorities and understanding how the process standards, such as higher order thinking and cooperative skills, weave into the fabric of the content. The real work of teachers is in aligning the standards to the curriculum they are required to teach and in the clustering of the standards with that curriculum content. Only through intricate texturing of the standards into complex student performances can the overwhelming number of standards be properly addressed. If teachers try to lay the standards end to end and approach them in some sequential manner, they will never reach the end of the line—there are simply too many standards for that direct approach to work effectively and efficiently.

Requiring middle school students to take on the role of newspaper publishers for a history unit about their hometown is the kind of complex task that illustrates how teachers layer and texture a cluster of standards. Within the task of creating a mock newspaper that depicts an era of history in the town, content standards involving historical data become the history content focus. Process standards of research skills, language usage, and written and oral communication skills are addressed as students interview and research and gather the facts of the times. The technology skills of word processing and graphic arts are integrated as students design and prepare the paper for publication.

In addition, the skills of teamwork and compromise and reaching agreements are interwoven in arriving at the final product. Significant "habits of mind," such as pride in one's work and persistence at a task, are bonus standards that are part of the robust performance requirements. This is how teachers design curriculum to meet student learning standards, not by addressing the standard as "the content." Complex performance tasks are compelling to students. Working on a standard by itself reduces the teaching/learning scenario to what is commonly known as "skill and drill." It's easy to discern which method students deserve. And it's easy to tell which method teachers prefer, if they are to meet the many standards on their agendas.

A Known Knowledge Base of Core Curriculum Content!

A first-year teacher confessed her worst nightmare to me in a letter about her concerns as a new professional. She said, plainly and painfully, "I have the standards and I have the curriculum materials, but I really don't know what I am supposed to teach. I know I can't do all of this, but I don't really know what is most important. I'm not sure how other teachers sort it all out and make sense of the curriculum."

This may seem a bit naïve to seasoned staff members, but if they think about a time they taught a new course or changed grade levels, they have a sense of what new teachers face as they try to make sense of the curriculum.

"What are the real priorities?" is the question that haunts the novices. How do they attack the avalanche of material before them? How do they begin to sort it out and set curricular priorities?

MAP THE COURSE—THEN TALK WITH AN EXPERT

The best way for new teachers to tackle the needed knowledge base and the core content is to review the curriculum guides, texts, and supplemental materials for the grade level or department. Teachers then need to identify and gather these resources as soon as possible, even before the term begins. Once the resources are in hand, new teachers need to survey the guides, skim and scan all the documents, and get a sense of the curriculum landscape. Then they need to make some preliminary notes, marking the units, topics, and concepts that comprise, in their judgment, the core content of the course or subject, which is the knowledge base that is basic and sentinel to learning. At the same time, the teachers should look over the standards again and think about how they integrate with the emerging curriculum scheme.

Armed with these notes of their first impression of the curricular priorities, new teachers should arrange to sit down with a willing colleague and discuss their ideas. They should compare thoughts, talk about priorities of the grade level or department, the length of time for various learning experiences, the depth of study anticipated, and the sequence and timing devoted to the core pieces. Then, new teachers can extract a semester or year-long schedule that synthesizes "the big picture." In essence, together they create a curriculum map for the term to use, literally, as a road map for instructional planning.

During the discussion, the new teachers should ask the experienced teacher questions about what and why and how. New teachers should elicit as much information as possible about how decisions are made. They must try to gain insight into why things are sorted out in certain ways and talk about "best and worst case" scenarios. They should ask, "What happens if . . . ? How might I . . . ? Why do you . . . ? What do you do when . . . ?" in anticipation of plausible situations.

This core curriculum model presents a two-pronged process: (1) developing an individual curriculum map and (2) sharing and comparing the initial ideas with another teacher. In this way, new teachers take the initial responsibility to dig into the curriculum on their own to discern the key concepts and at the same time share and compare their results with a knowing colleague. In addition, by beginning the conversation early in the term, the door is now open for continued dialogue as the curriculum unfolds. Eventually, this leads to confidence in a "known (identified, agreed to, and generally accepted) knowledge base" and a true understanding of the core curriculum content.

A Fail-Safe Lesson Design for Teachers to Teach and Learners to Learn!

Skillful teaching is inextricably linked to lesson design. It is the hallmark of excellent teachers. As architects of the intellect they know just how to lay out the plans for fail-safe lessons. They truly understand the delicacy of the equation inherent in the teaching/learning process. They know how to include the essential elements with expert input, how to use a wide variety of resources, how to structure "brain-friendly" learning experiences, how to include special needs students, how to give clear and concise instructions, and how to build accountability for student achievement. These architects know their craft well.

In the blueprints they work with, they tease the learner with an inviting sketch that lures the students to the scene (*anticipatory set*). These architects get the interest of their patrons (the students, in this case) and "hook" them into the learning in multiple ways. They may use teacher talk and well-worn stories, invite a surprise guest to appear before the class, show a specially selected video clip, embark on an excursion around the school grounds, or stage a role play to occur unexpectedly before an unknowing audience. Whatever they do, they do it deliberately and dramatically and with intent. Their purpose is to engage the minds of these young people and to capture the interest of their students.

These skillful architects then reveal the basic foundational pieces, giving students the core information and data they need to proceed (*input*). In this essential phase of the teaching/learning process, these architects design with great care. They share their understanding of their craft with simplicity and grace. They have studied their content so well that they know instinctively what is too much, what is not enough, and what is just the right amount of input for the learners to "get the stuff." They use every resource they have to construct a base that is solid and sound. They use textbook knowledge, graphs and charts, posterized renditions, expert testimony, analogies, and metaphorical references. They use the specialized, cognitive tools of the trade well.

Next, these craftsman of the classroom provide an exquisite model of the work with every detail in place (*modeling*). They unveil a three-dimensional model in all its glory, hoping to instruct and invite and inspire future genius in these waiting protégés. They narrate a "walking tour" of the model, exposing its staid traditions, fundamental ornaments, and uniquely mounted features. The model is the quintessential specimen to revel in and be revered. It is the model to aspire to.

TEACH THEM—THEN COACH THEM!

They then proceed with the design that brings the learner into the learning with intensely involving experiences. Students are structured into small, cooperative groups to encourage them to converse with each other in a collaborative effort. Teachers make a number of critical decisions in forming the cooperative teams. They must decide on the composition or make-up of the group, the size of the group (2–4), roles and responsibilities needed (Materials Manager, Recorder, Reporter, Encourager), the performance task, and how students are accountable for the learning. In these groups, students are expected to take responsibility as individuals and as a team, to problem solve and reach agreements, to produce, and to be individually accountable for the assignment. Giving step-by-step instructions, the architect scaffolds the learning for the willing apprentices (*guided practice*) as they undertake the tasks of the group. Each phase is carefully laid out and scrutinized by the master for accuracy and likeness to the reigning model. In addition, the process is carefully observed for later feedback for the teams.

Offering expert guidance and on-site coaching along the way (*monitoring and feedback*), the masters advise and mentor these earnest young minds. Students are queried about their work and groups are assisted as needed. The role of the master, at this point, is to guide and facilitate the work with specific feedback and coaching and continual encouragement. The knowing eye of the architect notices the subtleties of each design and leads the group to define, redefine, and refine the work they do. The process is as important as the product, for it is the process that takes them along the journey to the next assignment.

Soon, the apprentices seem ready. They have demonstrated their abilities in the basics, and they are encouraged to use those developing skills to create a design of their own (*independent practice*). The assignment might be an in-class project that extends over time or some daily work, on their own, that shows evidence of their learning, or it may be a homework assignment that demonstrates their individual understanding of the concepts and skills. The goal at this point in the lesson design is for the master architect to determine how capable these apprentices really are.

#8 A Repertoire of Teaching Strategies: Different Strokes for Different Folks!

A repertoire of teaching strategies means exactly that: a growing and ever-expanding repertoire of instructional methods—options that tap into the many ways students know and understand. However it's done, a repertoire means more than one!

The skillful teacher is aware of the differences in the students she or he teaches. Just think of the variety one finds in the physical development. There are tall students and short students; students with long hair and students with short hair; students who are full-bodied and those who are slight and slender; there are students who are left-handed, right-handed and even ambidextrous; there are students who are loud in their ways and those who try not to be noticed; there are students who are sleepy and those who are hungry.

Just as there are all these obvious and observable differences in the physical attributes of the students in a class, imagine the not-so-obvious and not-so-observable differences in the cognitive functioning of these same students. There are students who write easily and well and those who dread the written assignment; there are those who read fluently and with insight and there are others who have no clue; there are artistic types and others who are not able to visualize their thoughts; there are problem solvers and logical thinkers and others who would rather not have to deduce anything; there are youngsters who ride the waves of surround-sound music and those who have little or no connection to the melodies that often permeate the world of the musician. There are students who are athletically fit and excel at many sports and there are others who are always the last ones picked. There are students who lead and there are those who follow; there are youngsters who revel in self-reflection and know themselves to perfection and there are others who wonder aloud, "Who am I?" and "Where am I going?" Students are different, period. Learners are different . . . and that means they need different approaches.

TAP INTO THE TALENTS OF EACH LEARNER

Different strokes for different folks means any number of things to the skillful teacher. It means tapping Howard Gardner's theory and incorporating a multiple intelligences approach to the teaching/learning process, complementing the descriptions profiled earlier in this piece. It means using verbal, visual, bodily, musical, mathematical, inter and intra personal experiences, and the perspective of the naturalists who understand the flora and fauna of the natural environment (". . . eight is enough,").

Different strokes for different folks means differentiating the instruction in multiple ways: teachers can change the actual *content,* the learning *environment,* the instructional *process* or the requirements for the *product.* In so doing, teachers attempt to meet the spectrum of talents and gifts of the students they teach. Changing the content may mean offering a selection of novels to read that focus on a common theme, such as friendship. Students choose the novel of interest or the reading level that is most comfortable. Changing the learning environment means using the resource center for the students who need quiet or allowing others to work with headphones on, if they respond to music. Changing the process means letting some work in pairs for collaborative synergy and asking others to work as a team of four to accomplish individual tasks. Changing the product means encouraging students to use many ways of expressing what they know and are able to do as they present their information. They may use puppets, role plays, a newscast, radio talk show, written reports, or discussion groups.

Different strokes for different folks means problem-based learning, case studies, thematic instruction, projects, and service learning. It means performance learning, apprenticeships, internships, walkabouts and excursions in the field or virtual trips on-line. Differentiated instruction means distance learning, classroom learning, brain-based learning, and real-life learning. Differentiated learning means the teacher changes something to meet the needs, and sometimes the wants, of the learners.

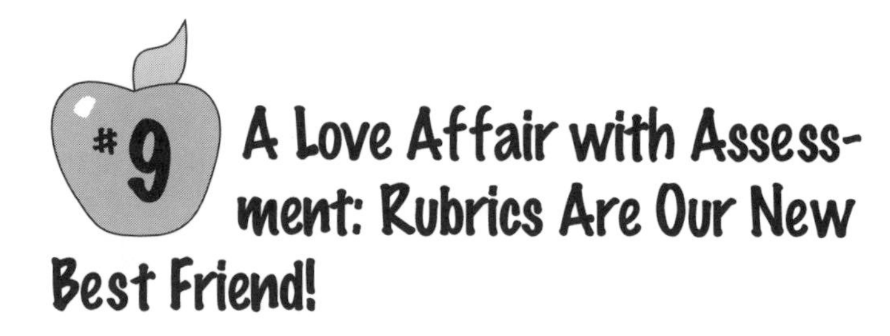

#9 A Love Affair with Assessment: Rubrics Are Our New Best Friend!

The cynics say, "Assessment drives instruction!", implying that all instructional decisions are governed by the assessment instruments that reign supreme in a district striving for excellence. When this culture thrives in a school, the teachers feel tremendous pressure to "raise the test scores." Unfortunately, the well-intentioned dictate that strives for higher student achievement often leads teachers away from the robust teaching models and toward more didactic methods that stress skill and drill exercises resembling test-taking scenarios. Teachers may, in the end, become focused on teaching to the test rather than teaching for a lifetime.

Another way to think about assessment, and perhaps a more accurate observation of the process, is summed up in the saying, "Assessment is instruction! Instruction is assessment!" Assessment, when designed as authentic student performances, creates a need for what is called "backward design of curriculum and instruction." Therefore, based on the standards or goals, teachers decide what it is that students need to know and be able to do. Next, teachers think about what evidence signifies that students know something and are able to do whatever it is they are expected to do. Finally, teachers think about how they might judge the quality of the student learning. In other words, the assessment involves three distinct elements that are inextricably linked to instruction: the *standard* of learning, the *evidence* of that learning, and the *judgment* about the quality of learning. Once these interwoven elements are clearly in mind, the teacher is able to design the learning in an informed and skillful way. Therefore, assessment does become instruction.

SHARE CRITERIA FOR SUCCESS WITH STUDENTS BEFORE THEY BEGIN THE TASK

And the reverse is true, also, because instruction that requires students to demonstrate what they know and what they are able to do is instruction that has the assessment built in. This is performance assessment in all its glory, and it is the essence of instructional methods that dictate performance tasks or authentic evidence and judgment (rubric) of the learning. The analogy might read like this:

> Evidence is to Judgment as Performance Task is to Rubric.

In this equation, assessment requires *evidence* of the learning and, in turn, ways to judge that evidence in terms of the quality of that performance. This *judgment* of the *performance task* is best assessed through the use of a scoring guide or a *rubric*. In this way, the student performance is critiqued against criteria and indicators of how well the criteria are met.

For example, a *standard* of learning may state:

> Students are able to demonstrate understanding and application of the principles of geometry.

To design curriculum and instruction that require students to show how well they understand and can apply one principle of geometry, the teacher might design a project learning unit. In this way, students can demonstrate their learning through the instructional experience, showing how the Pythagorean theorem and its 3, 4, 5 relationship helps to square a model structure. Working as partners or small cooperative groups, students can be required to build two models. In one design the students can show a structure constructed using the "right triangle design" based on the theorem and that the structure is square. With the squareness comes quality. In a comparable design, they can demonstrate the lack of squareness when the "right triangle" structure is not used and they can demonstrate the inferior quality of the structure. Thus, the performance task or the evidence is provided.

Now the teacher must judge the quality of the performance through the use of a scoring guide or rubric. This requires criteria and indicators of how well the criteria are met. Criteria for the project might include both content and process standards which would be recorded in the first vertical column. Indicators of the quality of the performance are shown in the top horizontal line. Parallel indicators across the horizontal lines comprise indicators in the rubric. Figure 1 shows a blank rubric template.

Rubric Title				
Criteria/Indicators	**Not Evident**	**Developing**	**Competent**	**Proficient**

Figure 1: Rubric Template

In summary, to think of assessment as instruction and instruction as assessment, teachers use "the backward design" method for curriculum and instruction. In this way, teachers incorporate the standards of learning, the evidence of learning, and the judgment of the quality of the learning in complex tasks that engage students in the teaching/learning process. Thus, the assessment/instruction conundrum is solved in one glorious project. At last!

#10 A Winning Way with Parents: To Report, Relate, and Celebrate

It's plain and simple. Teachers and students benefit when parents are involved in the teaching/learning process. That involvement comes in a variety of ways: formal and informal reporting to parents; engagement of parents in volunteer work in the classroom and/or in the school; and invitations to parents to share in student performances and celebrations of student achievement.

Formal reporting to parents is usually through the use of report cards, parent conferences, meetings between school personnel and the parents and official phone calls to parents about students. When these formal communications occur, it is wise for teachers to remember one overriding goal: Let the parent talk, too! There is little real communication happening if the teacher is doing all the talking. Teachers need to invite the parents to participate in the process and let them share their impressions first. Teachers might elicit responses from parents as the dialogue, not the monologue, unfolds. Whenever possible and appropriate, teachers often invite the student to be a part of the conversation, also. After all, it is in the student's best interest, as the topic of the conversation, to take some ownership in the process.

INVOLVE PARENTS IN THE TEACHING/LEARNING PROCESS

Informal ways of communicating and reporting to parents might include the following: a class newsletter to parents depicting past and future events; weekly or sometimes even daily notes on student papers and projects; memos to parents about special events; and unique notes that communicate "little successes" and "little concerns" that just keep the parent informed and up-to-date on students' lives at school. One teacher created two forms on half sheets of ditto paper: one was the Yea! Yea!, the other was the Oops! The Yea! Yea! went home when students did something to cheer about: finished a book, got an A on the spelling test, helped someone who was hurt, shared lunch with a friend, or came up with a great question that day. The Oops! went home when students did something of concern, something that did not seem too serious but warranted a "heads up" for the parents: pushing in the lunch line, not completing a daily assignment, disrupting another group, demonstrating poor manners in the assembly. While the tenor of these frequent communications changes with the age groups of the students, the intent remains the same. The teacher must take the initiative to stay in touch with the parents. By using these notes, parents have frequent communication from the teacher that is both positive and negative. It opens the lines of communication and keeps them open if parents are required to sign the notes and return them to the teacher.

And here's an "information age" idea. Teachers might create a class web site to carry massive amounts of information about the topics under study, upcoming events, instructions about how parents might help with the homework, or information about educational issues of concern and relevance. Depending on the age of the students, they might even create the web site and take responsibility for maintaining it.

In addition to formal and informal communication with parents, there are opportunities to engage parents in actual volunteer work in the school classroom. They make great reading partners in the young grades, or willing helpers on field trips, picnics, and other school excursions. In one classroom, the teacher invited a team of parents to come in and assist students with a simple machine unit in which each student had to build a dragon with moveable parts. The parent team served to help the students who might not have had a parent at home to help them. In the upper grades, parents can participate in similar ways with complex projects, field trips, clerical duties, or even as guest speakers in an area of expertise. The more the parents are linked to the classroom activities, the better their understanding of what the teaching/learning process is all about.

One final way of involving parents is by inviting them into the classroom for various performances, celebrations, or culminating events to a unit of study. This strategy of getting parents to the school is usually a no-fail method, as every parent wants to see his or her student perform. And, of course, the students put some pressure on the parents to show up—that helps the cause, too.

Everyone benefits when the parents are involved in classroom events, school issues, and student activities. It is the winning way!

Bibliography

Introduction

Peter, L. I. 1977. *Peter's quotations: Ideas for our time.* New York: Morrow.

Pirsig, R. M. 1984. *Zen and the art of motorcycle maintenance.* New York: Bantam Books.

Strunk, W. J., and White, E. B. 2000. *The elements of style.* 4th ed. Needham Heights, MA: Allyn and Bacon.

1. Mentor and Colleague

Ashton-Warner, S. 1986. *Teacher.* New York: Simon & Schuster.

Blanchard, K. 1993. *The one minute manager.* Berkley Publishing Group.

Codell, E. R. 1999. *Educating Esme: Diary of a teacher's first year.* Algonquin Books.

Johnson, S. 1998. *Who moved my cheese?* Putnam Publishing Group.

Schmuck, R., and Schmuck, P. 2000. *Group processes in the classroom.* Dubuque, IA: WCB/McGraw-Hill.

2. The Classroom

Bloom, B. 1981. *All our students learning.* New York: McGraw-Hill.

Costa, A. 1991. *The school as a home for the mind.* Arlington Heights, IL: IRI/SkyLight Training and Publishing, Inc.

Csikszentmihalyi, M. 1990. *Flow: The psychology of optimal experience.* New York: Harper & Row.

Diamond, M., and Hopson, J. 1999. *Magic trees of the mind.* Penguin USA.

Goleman, D. 1997. *Emotional intelligence.* New York: Bantam Books.

Goodlad, J. I. 1994. *A place called school.* New York: McGraw-Hill.

Lewkowicz, A. B. 1999. *Teaching emotional intelligence: Making informed choices.* Arlington Heights, IL: SkyLight Training and Publishing Inc.

3. Classroom Management

Block, J., and Anderson, L. W. 1975. *Mastery learning in classroom instruction.* New York: Macmillan.

Bosch, K. 1999. *Planning classroom management for change.* Arlington Heights, IL: SkyLight Training and Publishing Inc.

Guskey, T. R., ed. 1994. *High-stakes performance assessment: Perspectives on Kentucky's educational reform.* Thousand Oakes, CA: Corwin Press, Inc. A Sage Publications Company.

Hunter, M. 1971. *Teach for transfer.* El Segundo, CA: TIP Publications.

Joyce, B., and Weil, M. 2000. *Models of Teaching.* 6th ed. Needham Heights, MA: Allyn and Bacon.

4. Discipline

Burke, K. 2000. *What to do with the kid who . . .* 2nd ed. Arlington Heights, IL: SkyLight Training and Publishing Inc.

Evertson, C., Emmer, E. T., Clements, B. S., and Worsham, M. E. 1997. *Classroom management for elementry teachers.* Boston: Allyn & Bacon.

Jones, V. F., and Jones, L. S. 1998. *Comprehensive classroom management: Creating communities of support and solving problems.* 5th ed. Boston: Allyn and Bacon.

Wolfgang, C. H. 1999. *Solving discipline problems: Methods and models for today's teachers.* 4th ed. Boston: Allyn and Bacon.

5. Standards

Burke, K. 1999. *The mindful school: How to assess authentic learning.* 3rd ed. Arlington Heights, IL: SkyLight Training and Publishing Inc.

Marzano, R., and Kendall, J. S. 1996. *A comprehensive guide to designing standards-based districts, schools, and classrooms.* Alexandria, VA: ASCD and Mid-Continent Regions Educational Laboratory.

Perna, D., and Davis, J. 2000. *Aligning standards and curriculum for classroom success.* Arlington Heights, IL: SkyLight Training and Publishing Inc.

Wiggins, G., and McTighe, J. 1998. *Understanding by design.* Alexandria, VA: ASCD.

6. Curriculum

Beane, J., ed. 1995. *Toward a coherent curriculum: 1995 yearbook of the ASCD.* Alexandria, VA: ASCD.

Fogarty, R. 1991. *The mindful school: How to integrate the curricula.* Arlington Heights, IL: IRI/SkyLight Training and Publishing, Inc.

Fogarty, R., and Stoehr, J. 1995. *Integrating the curricula with multiple intelligences: Teams, themes and threads.* Arlington Heights, IL: IRI/SkyLight Training and Publishing, Inc.
Jacobs, H. 1990. *Interdisciplinary Curriculum: Design and Implementation.* Alexandria, VA: ASCD.

7. Lesson Design

Fogarty, R. 1994. *The mindful school: How to teach for metacognitive reflection.* Arlington Heights, IL: IRI/SkyLight Training and Publishing, Inc.
———. 1997. *Brain-compatible classrooms.* SkyLight Training and Publishing Inc.
———. In Press. "Architects of the Intellect" in *Developing minds: A resource book for teaching thinking.* 2nd Edition Ed. Art Costa. Alexandria, VA: Association for Supervision and Curriculum Development.
Johnson, D., Johnson, R., and Holubec, E. J. 1986. *Circles of learning: Cooperation in the classroom.* Alexandria, VA: ASCD.
Kagan, S. 1992. *Cooperative learning structures.* San Clemente, CA: Kagan Cooperative.
Perkins, D. 1992. *Smart schools: From training memories to educating minds.* New York: Free Press.
———. 1995. *Outsmarting IQ: The emerging science of learnable intelligence.* New York: Free Press.
Skowron, J. 2001. *Powerful lesson planning models.* SkyLight Taining and Publishing Inc.
Slavin, R. 1983. *Cooperative learning.* New York: Longman.

8. Teaching Repertoire

Berman, S. 1999. *Service learning for the multiple intelligences classroom.* Arlington Heights, IL: Skylight Training and Publishing Inc.
Fogarty, R. 1997. *Problem-based learning and other curriculum models for the multiple intelligences classroom.* Arlington Heights, IL: IRI/SkyLight Training and Publishing, Inc.
Gardner, H. 1983. *Frames of mind: The theory of multiple intelligences.* New York: Basic Books.
———. 1993. *Multiple intelligences: The theory in practice.* New York: HarperCollins.
Joyce, B., and Weil, M. 2000. *Models of teaching.* 6th ed. Needham Heights, MA: Allyn and Bacon.

Kovalic, S. 1993. *ITI: The model: Integrated thematic instruction.* Village of Oak Creek, AZ: Books for Educators.

Tomilson, C. A. 1999. *The differentiated classroom: Responding to the needs of all learners.* Alexandria, VA: ASCD.

9. Assessment

Burke, K. 1999. *The mindful school: How to assess authentic learning.* 3rd ed. Arlington Heights, IL: SkyLight Training and Publishing Inc.

Burke, K., Fogarty, R., and Belgrad, S. 1994. *The mindful school: The portfolio connection.* Arlington Heights, IL: IRI/SkyLight Publishing, Inc.

Fogarty, R. 1998. *Balanced assessment.* Arlington Heights, IL: SkyLight Training and Publishing Inc.

———. 1999. *How to raise test scores.* Arlington Heights, IL: SkyLight Training and Publishing Inc.

O'Connor, K. 1999. *The mindful school: How to grade for learning.* Arlington Heights, IL: SkyLight Training and Publishing, Inc.

Popham, W. J. 1999. *Classroom assessment: What teachers need to know.* 2nd. ed. Boston: Allyn and Bacon.

Stiggins, R. 1994. *Student-centered classroom assessment.* New York: MacMillan College Publishing.

10. Parents

Burke, K. 1999. *The mindful school: How to assess authentic learning.* 3rd ed. Arlington Heights, IL: SkyLight Training and Publishing Inc.

Burke, K., Fogarty, R., and Belgrad, S. 1994. *The mindful shool: The portfolio connection.* Arlington Heights, IL: IRI/SkyLight Publishing, Inc.

Schiller, D. P., and Caroll, M. K. 1986. *A research-based approach to improving instruction.* Oxford, OH: National Staff Development Council.

Walberg, H. L. 1984. Families as partners in educational productivity. *Phi Delta Kappan* 65(6): 397–400.